THIS BOOK BELONGS TO:

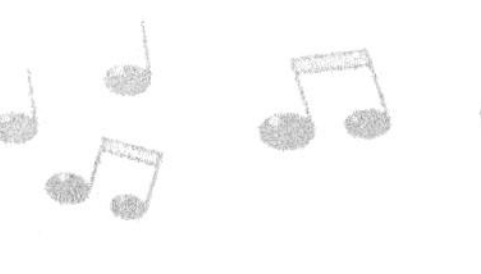

Copyright 2020
GRB Journals Publishing

I LOVE YOU
BECAUSE
YOU ARE

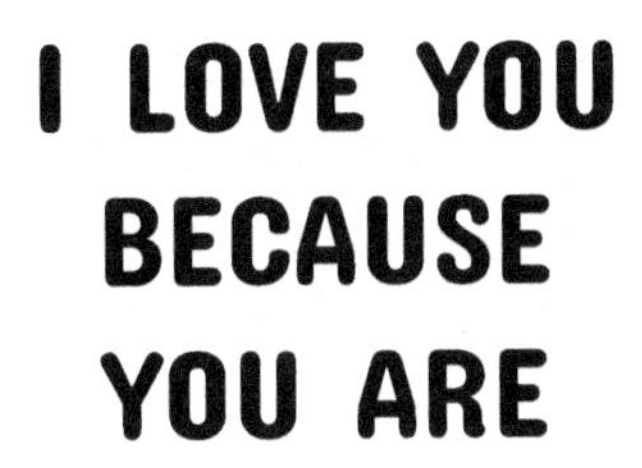

YOU ARE THE WORLD'S BEST

I LOVE IT
WHEN YOU

I LOVE YOUR

YOU ARE MY

YOU LOVE IT
WHEN WE

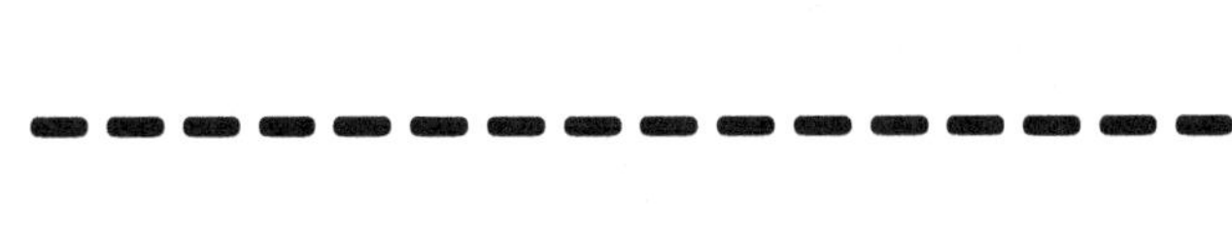

YOU ARE MY
FAVORITE

YOU ARE A VERY GOOD

YOU ARE SUCH
A NICE

YOU ALWAYS
HELP ME TO

I LIKE IT
WHEN YOU COOK

____

____

I LOVE IT WHEN
YOU LET ME

YOU LOVE MY

YOU FORGAVE ME
WHEN I

____

____

IT'S SO FUNNY
WHEN YOU

YOU LOVE IT
WHEN I

- - - - - - - - - - - - - - - - - - -

- - - - - - - - - - - - - - - - - - -

YOUR ARE NOT AFRAID TO

YOU TOOK ME TO

YOU BOUGHT ME A

YOU TAUGHT ME HOW TO

____

____

YOU DIDN'T GET MAD
WHEN I

YOU LISTENED TO ME
WHEN I

YOU HAVE THE BEST

YOU ARE BETTER
THAN A

____

____

YOU ARE THERE WHEN I

____

____

YOU ARE
MY HERO BECAUSE

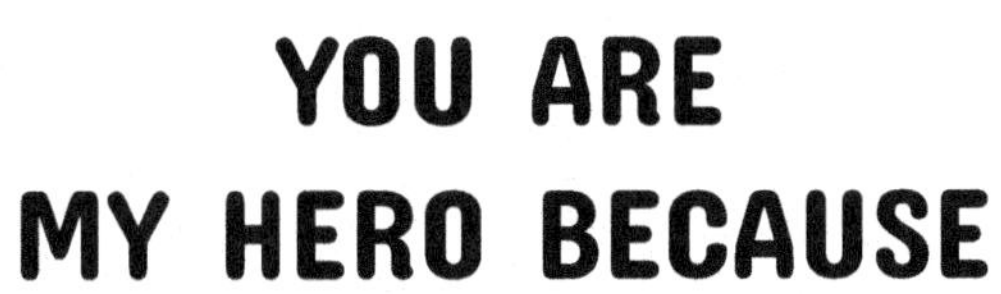

____

____

YOU ARE
THE BEST

MY FAVORITE
GIFT FROM YOU IS

____

____

I LAUGHED SO MUCH
WHEN YOU

_ _ _ _ _ _ _ _ _ _ _ _ _ _ _ _ _

_ _ _ _ _ _ _ _ _ _ _ _ _ _ _ _ _

IT'S SO FUNNY
WHEN YOU